BEAR TRACKS

BEAR TRACKS

MEMORIES OF A HO-CHUNK ELDER

SHERMAN FUNMAKER

WISCONSIN HISTORICAL SOCIETY PRESS

Published by the Wisconsin Historical Society Press
Publishers since 1855

The Wisconsin Historical Society helps people connect to the past by collecting, preserving, and sharing stories. Founded in 1846, the Society is one of the nation's finest historical institutions.
Join the Wisconsin Historical Society: wisconsinhistory.org/membership

All interior photos used courtesy of Sherman Funmaker and the Funmaker–Stacy family.
Front cover: Image of the Dells of the Wisconsin River from a historic postcard in the Wisconsin Historical Society collections, WHi Image ID 151576. Photo of the author courtesy of Sherman Funmaker and the Funmaker-Stacy family.

Printed in the United States of America
Cover designed by Steve Biel
Typesetting by John Ferguson

30 29 28 27 26   1 2 3 4 5

Library of Congress Cataloging-in-Publication Data available.

♾ The paper used in this publication meets the minimum requirements of the American National Standard for Information Sciences—Permanence of Paper for Printed Library Materials, ANSI Z39.48-1992.

To my parents, Adam and Doris,
Brothers Gary, Ira, Martin, and Nathaniel,
Sisters Lois, Ada, Ila, Myra, Mona, Rita, and Fran.
For all my relatives and friends.

A drawing of me made by my dad, Adam (Yellow Horse) Funmaker. He was a talented artist.

Contents

Recording

Whisper me
One more time
Tell the story
Of us
How we broke
Like glass on floors
Shattered bloody
Lying there
Waiting to be
Swept away
Breathless panic
Confines
A weakened mind
Too tired
To fight
The pool of blood
Reflects the love
That drips along
The tile walk
Washed away
On rainy nights
Shadows crawl
Toward Moon's
Gravity
Just in time
To record
What happened
On Earth

Introduction

I never thought about school when I was growing up. My early days as a student left a bad taste in my mouth. Being a brown kid, I felt left out of things and was picked on. The teachers didn't stick up for me. I didn't see how school would help with my quest to be a rock drummer, so I got out as soon as I could. I dropped out when I was sixteen. My mom seemed to be okay with that, although I perceived my dad was not in agreement. I was a stubborn kid and wasn't aware of how my actions affected my family.

My folks never talked about education, politics, or our futures. They were busy raising eleven kids with as much love as we needed. They probably thought we would figure it out as we went. And, eventually, we all did. I left home as a teenager and went west to pursue music with my band. I didn't have a plan, just a dream to perform with my friends. I spent years outside of Wisconsin drumming, creating, and growing. Then I came home.

In 2002, I decided to visit the university right down the road from where I lived. With help from UW–Baraboo and the Ho-Chunk Nation, I started my college career, something I never thought I would do. I learned that I liked being in the classroom, meeting new people, and using my brain. My education plan didn't include any kind of writing. I started off as a business major, but eventually writing became a larger part of my school life, and I left business behind.

Before my university days, I may have written three letters in my whole life. Nowadays, I love writing about something or someone that means a lot to me. I love waiting for the words to come to me. I had always heard people say, "If I can do it, so can you."

When I give talks now, I end up saying that very thing because I believe it's true.

Working on this book has taken me back to when I was a kid. It has gotten me thinking about my family and the lives we have led to this point—the good and the bad, happy times and sad times. It has made me appreciate what we have and the ways the Lord has had his hand on us during this journey.

I have given talks at schools and universities and mentored Ho-Chunk kids, but I never thought of sharing my writing. For me, writing is a form of therapy. I write down thoughts and send them out to the universe. I miss the people I have loved, and writing about them allows me to visit them when I need to. The memory of those who have gone on is a treasure in my heart. Having my words put into a book is more than I ever imagined would happen. I began writing in 2003, and many pieces in this book were created back then. I don't want to be famous or rich. I don't want to be considered some sort of artist. I am a blessed man who has lived a life full of ups and downs and managed to come out alive. These words are reflections of those experiences, and I am glad I get to share them with you.

My People All Around

That's me. A kid in a little Wisconsin town, one of eleven. Child of two strong, loving Native American parents. Trying to make sense of all that was going on. It wasn't easy living in a big family. We had some rough times, but my folks did their best to provide for us.

We can't choose who our parents and family are, but I would never change how I came into this world. We were loved and cared for, and as far as we knew, we were a good fit in the world around us.

Third Kid

The Black River floated by
As the world welcomed another Indian
One of eleven sounds pretty crowded
And it was, growing up surrounded
By the land
My people came to love
For me, it was the beginning of my journey
Called on from above
I don't remember much
As I was carried around
Being a home-grown red boy
Being taken into town
I grew up with strong women
My mom and her mom led me
Guided me through the first few years
Hoping they would get me
The world was strange as I grew up and saw
How the white world was
Hate and colors blinded red
I'm glad I saw those days ahead
When I go back to that little town
I picture my people all around
Those who passed and left a mark
On my life and on my heart

Mother's Day

She was the enforcer in the family
No one gave her any lip
She loved the ones she loved
And if she didn't like you, you knew it
She grew up tough
In a time when you needed to be
She brought us up like a strong woman would
We loved and respected her
She never failed us
Provided for all our needs
By hook or by crook, she always did what she had to do
She took me to my auditions
Was my biggest fan
My bodyguard, my roadie, my mom
I felt safe when she was near
No one could hurt me

The Busy Bee

My mom and pops always found
The neighborhood greasy spoon
Mauston town had a good one
Small-town haven with little room
My folks were old school and that was fine
The greasier the better
I think they felt at home in those places
Drinking coffee and eating eggs
Bargain meals on the board
Nothing fancy here
There aren't many of those left now
Big chain cafes taking their place
No more small-town places for moms and pops
Those were the good old days
Good unhealthy food on the menu

Cry Baby Totem

Yes, this is me
sitting up on a tree
I don't remember how old I was
And me crying hard I don't wanna discuss
I guess I was afraid of high places
I could think of more comfortable spaces
I think I was maybe five or six years
Scared out of my mind
Thus shedding the tears

Who put me up there?

The Old Days

We were so close
The family I love
The days went by fast
With help from above
We weren't dressed the best
And that was okay
Our lives were in the process of living
And giving . . .
Not concerned with what was going on around us
The days were slow
No internet to distract us
Playing outside all day long
Climbing trees and riding bikes
Gone until the sun went down
Not worried about someone taking us
I mean, who would want a dirty Indian boy
Who eats like there's no tomorrow?
Gathered together to watch one TV
The phone party line
Spying on neighbors
Broke up boring nights

If we were poor
We didn't really notice
Too busy having fun
And not keeping up with the Joneses
Seems like just a few days ago
Mom and Dad keeping us safe
And us
Watching it all pass by

Indian Baptist Church

My folks took us there
Almost every Sunday
It was nice to hear the people sing
Some a bit out of tune
That was okay
It felt real
A little church in the middle of nowhere
Those songs that rang true
In our hearts and in our souls
They stayed in my mind
And in my young boy heart
The gospel sank in to my heart
Songs of Heaven
Songs of love and happiness
It's still there to this day
The little church I will always remember
Family and friends are buried there
Around the pines that cast soft shade
I miss those days when Mom and Dad
Would take us for sweets after
We shook hands at the door of the church
Headed out into the world
Feeling a little closer to family
Closer to God

Poor Boy's Life

It wasn't like we knew it
Not having . . . things
It wasn't all that bad
Now that I look back

We were brown in a white world
I finally figured that out, but it took me a while
I really wasn't thinking about it

It was life as we knew it
The way it was
Good times still came around
And kept us under family love

Good times, bad times
Like everyone else on this planet
They come and go like sunup and down
I think it made us closer
Thicker and clearer
It made us strong

Hard times?
Yeah, but that is the way of the world
Only the strong survive
That's what they keep telling me

I attended grade school in Lyndon Station. I recall the day my mom drove me there, handed me my lunch, and waved goodbye. There I was, alone and scared among strangers. I remember the teacher's name and that she made me feel okay as I looked out the window to see if my mom would return to rescue me.

Little White Schoolhouse

I don't remember what grade that was
My memory has been on hold
For quite a while
I think I hated every day there
People staring at the poor Indian boy
Ragged jeans and an oversized shirt
And wishing I were home
I looked out the window to see if my mom was there
She left, rode off without a sound
Left me in the dust of that little town.
As long as I can remember
I hated school . . . I mean *hated*
My dad had to throw me on a bus or two
Dragging my dumb ass across the lawn
With grass-stained jeans I went to school
Couldn't wait to get out of there
Not that I was dumb
I have a high IQ
Whatever that is

I was bored and I figured I didn't need
To know more than reading
And writing, cooking some food
I guess I was wrong
I have a degree now
I sat through class and got a sheet that
Says I do
Take that,
Little white schoolhouse

My cousin Joe Stacy was like a brother to me. We grew up together and had many adventures—good times and crazy times. He passed years ago. I miss him still.

Brothers

Looking back, brothers we were
In the cousin way
The times we spent together
The ones that I can remember
Summers in the Dells
Up to no good
Like the rest of the people
Not a care in the world
Enjoying being Indians
Running in the woods
Climbing and falling in trees
Swimming in the rivers
Washing up and sun drying
Along the mighty Wisconsin
Nighttime parties, drinking hard
And fighting
Those were the days
I miss them
And those who are still here

Branch

Twisted and torn
Like the branch
We sat on
When we were nine
Struck by lightning
That left its mark
On a couple of kids
Who knew no better
Than to stay and watch
Could have been us
That dried up and died
Stupid youth we were
One day in July
Never seeing what we
Would become
Alone again and hoping
The tree was still standing

When I was about twelve, my dad sent me to pick up my mom from Lyndon Station. I didn't have a license to drive, but back then no one seemed to care. We had a '57 Chevy that I had driven before but never on such a journey across Juneau County.

Driving to Lyndon

Twelve years old and my dad sent me out
A crosstown drive I won't forget
Picking up mom from family and friends

I didn't have the state's okay
Didn't bother anyone on that Saturday
Pop's '57 Chevy under my flops

Four on the floor
Was what I hoped for
But three on the tree was a little challenge
Small feet didn't help at all
Stretched out toes barely held on

The road seemed bigger
When I wasn't looking
Crossed the yellow line a time or two
Steering wheel hard to see over

WLS on my pop's radio
Kool cigarette hanging off my lip
I felt like a cool guy finally
All I needed was a pompadour hair style
Flying in the wind

Those were the days
Flying down the road
Without a care in the world

Feeling like *the man*
Who finally arrived
At his destination and
Can't wait for the next illegal adventure

My mom and my sister Lois ready to perform at the 1964 Indian Ceremonial in Wisconsin Dells

Stand Rock Indians

1919 was when they say it started
But we were dancing way before then
Along the river Wisconsin and in our hearts
The drums and voices echo in my head
The kid who watched them dance
Wishing I could do that
Performers from all over Indian Country
Came north to be a part of history
Entertained the crowd that came all summer long
When I think of the ones that are no more
They danced, they sang, they were close to the Earth
Leaving memories along the way
We went a bunch when I was a kid
My sister and relatives performed nightly
I love the songs and the dances that I couldn't do
I tried, but two left feet won't work

’60s Surf and Indians

Back before big brother saw us all
We sat in theaters Saturday afternoons
The cool kids sat in the front
Necks strained eyes wide open
Dreaming of LA
Peaceful beatniks inside my head
Wishing I was far from this lonely little town
Visions of beaches and blondes
Danced in my head
Far from where I grew up
Far from where I came from
Oh, how I wished my life
Was like silly, stupid movies
Dancing on white hot sand
Flipping my hair
Driving my woody
Matinees were my escape
Only for a moment . . . I was white
Tanned and surfing
Girls all around
Sea salt burns my eyes
Like the sun that made me brown

My grandma Stella Stacy

Stella Stacy, also known as Mountain Wolf Woman, was my mom's mother. We lived with her in Black River Falls, where I was born, in what is known as the Mission, a small settlement of Ho-Chunk people. Her house was always full of wonderful smells and activity. She cooked on a woodburning stove, grew crops, collected rainwater, and tanned deer hides.

My mom was her youngest, and they were very close. Both women were a big part of my life when I was a young child. I still feel that closeness to my mother and grandmother daily. They faced each day with the hope of bringing happiness to everyone they came across.

My grandmother Stella Stacy was born in April 1884 at her maternal grandfather's home in East Fork River, Wisconsin. She was the youngest of seven children born to Charles Blowsnake and Lucy Goodvillage. Although she was born a member of her father's Thunder clan, she was later given the Wolf clan name Xéhachiwinga. The Wolf clan is considered holy due to its wealth of healers.

Mountain Wolf Woman

My mom's mom was a strong lady
She was not famous, didn't want to be
Her life was full of love and prayers
Raising kids and living
Tanning hides, collecting rainwater
Before it was illegal
The stories of her life
Put down by anthropologists
That put her up and ran a tape
The stories that broke her heart
Told by open fires
She closed her eyes and spoke of life
Love and family always there
She took care of all that crossed her path
Talked of God and caring
My mom took it hard when she left this world
Held her tight from that day on

I only hope I can be
Like the one who prayed over me
Rocking in her chair
Shedding a lonely tear
We miss them more than we thought we would
The women in our lives
The ones who stood
For something
Bigger than who they were
Wanting us to relive the old days
Before the world turned to hate and war
It was a simpler time
And I have those memories
That make me feel like I came from
Women who were strong

2

All the Noise I Wanted

That's me on the right, hanging out with some
of the musicians I played with in Madison
in a band called Zapata, around 1968

I dropped out of high school in my sophomore year. Back then you could quit school at sixteen, and I jumped on it. I played drums in a three-piece band around home for a while and ended up in Madison a short time later. Music was all around, and I played with whoever I could. I had no money, no phone, no driver's license, and no bills. It was the best of times.

I stayed around Madison until November 1971, when I hitchhiked to California. The journey of a lifetime began.

February 1964

I was one of the millions
Who sat and watched that Sunday night
All of us sitting around
Kids scattered on the floor
Small town dreams
Woke up that day
Indian kid's head was screaming
I knew that was what I wanted
No matter what it took
From that day on
Practice makes perfect
That's what my pops said
They never complained about the noise I made
Every day after school
Beating on the cheap Ludwig set
Knowing it was what I dreamed of
No one understood and that was okay
It was the thing that kept burning in my heart
Nights I stayed in
Only going out to see the
One I'm with now
I kept it up
And never looked back
All because of those four guys
And the screaming that followed
I never got the screams . . . but that was okay

I got much more than that
My mom and dad cheered me on
Taking me to practice, being my first roadies
Letting me make all the noise I wanted
It made me what I am today
An old fart who still dreams of being on stage

My folks weren't musical people, other than listening to songs on the radio in the car. But my dad liked the old crooners, and I remember listening to Frank Sinatra with him. They don't make music like that anymore.

Dad and Frank

They were there on the jukebox and in my mind
Songs that for some reason
Made so much sense to me
How I wish I knew those tunes would get me through hard
  times later
That smooth voice that rang true in my head
My little brain full of questions of life and love
Why would they matter to an eight-year-old kid?
I felt good every time I heard them
Now they take me back to a better time
Before all the cares of this life
Stuck their ugly face before my easy eyes
I wish I could recall those tunes and memories
Bringing me to tears when I wasn't looking
Melodies that made me think
Of the beautiful girl
The songs were talking about

My dad and Frank are long gone now
But in my head
They are here every time I hum along
Those tunes that made me think of love
And life
Melodies and how they string me along

Heartbreak Hotel

The seven-inch vinyl turned around my head
Back in the day when I thought I was cool
Not as cool as I thought I was
Even for a five-year-old rebel
The music moved me
Like I never felt before
The black disc magic
Made me want to sing and dance
That little kitchen with one bulb hanging down
Felt like a dance floor beneath my feet
Every step closer to the sounds in my head
His hair was black and pompadour slick
I thought he was the coolest, for a white guy
This Indian kid's dream
Today it's still there
In my head and in my heart
The sounds that made me feel like I could dream and perform
It came to pass a few years later
Twelve years old and knowing this is what I want to do
Dropping school didn't bother me
I hated being told what to do
Garage band stinking up the neighborhood
Making noise only we thought was good
Making music without a care in the world

Dropout

I was sick of being told what to do
Rebel blood flowed through this kid
As long as I can remember
Taking orders wasn't my thing
Especially from white people that didn't like brownies
At the tender age of sixteen
I left that place behind
It was legal to drop out then
That's all I needed to know
I was out of that little town in no time
Off to Madtown and on to something more
I was a music man from the day I was born
It seemed to help me cope with this world
From what I could see all around me
Everyone needed something
I tried my best to sing everything I could
Not very good but good enough for now
I mean, it's rock 'n' roll . . .
You don't need to be good

Just pretend no one is listening

My mom, Doris Stacy Funmaker, began driving me to gigs when I was around sixteen.

The Roadie

My radio put me to sleep most nights
Chicago, Little Rock, and Oklahoma City
AM stations that kept me aware
Of what was going on outside my little world
They made me think of dreams that seemed so far away
Starting out on pots and pans
Banging my way into the world
Tunes that went on inside my head
Telling me stories, leading me on
The garage housed more than a car
Tinny and out of tune kids
Little amps pumped out top 40
Dreams of lights and music rocked us softly
She hauled my kit
Set it up and let me do my thing
Too young to drive but old enough to see the plan
My mom was my biggest fan
Always gave me what I needed
Dried my tears and held me tight
Letting me know
There was so much more to life
The songs I sang were of love and peace
Made me feel like nothing else did
This Indian kid found his place
In the world so sad and so full of hate

I am told that when I was very young, I would hum along with songs and almost always could recall lyrics. At some point, I started making drum noises with my mouth. Sounds cute, right? My dad sometimes saw it as a nuisance and would allow me to go on for only a few measures and then suggest I knock it off. I still did it, but it stayed in my head. Until I got behind a real drum set.

Saturday Night Lives

The little stage
Where we used to sing
Basketballs sit silent in the corner
Long gone and turned into a faint memory, those days
Like a whisper that flew through the night
Those days we wish we could relive

Still inside my head and clearly in my ear
Every time I hear our song
The one that makes me sort of dance
Two left feet was how I saw myself
She could twirl like no one's business

With a splash of soda and a shot of brandy
Sitting up there hiding behind cymbals and sweat
I used up all my strength and joy
Beating the hell out of both barrels—my toys

Those were the days
Not a care in the world
No car, no bills, no phones, and no one telling me what to do
Streets that were my home

Hitching back to where my hat hung
Inside a little house full of noisy kids
I was always glad to see them
And them to see me

Rockin the '60s

We were just punk kids
Rockin on weekends
In the garage or in our heads
Always ready to plug in and play
Hoping to rock the night away
We packed a van with our stuff
Smokin and jokin was never enough
It was a dream come true
For some small town guys
Who had no clue

Fuzzy pics for free

There I am, blurry in the background,
drumming my heart out.

GFR

Grand Funk Railroad was one of my faves
My little crappy garage band
Tried to do their songs justice
But when you get three small-town kids
Trying to make their way through the '60s music scene
We probably made fools of ourselves

But I didn't care
I loved being on stage
Loved everything about it
We never made money, I wasn't in it for money
It was my calling
I had no choice
That's what made it fun

Banging and singing my guts out
That's what I did every chance I had
With a coke and a hit of blackberry brandy
I had just enough buzz to keep rocking

The Summer of Love

Back in the day
This kid's head was in the clouds
All this stuff going on around me
In my house, in the world, and in my life

Wars all around
In my house, in my world, and in my life
Brown people were being mistreated
Death was making its way across the planet
White men walked on the Moon
I still can't remember that day

Streets were filled with kids making a statement
And good music was being made
And the Summer of Love
Kids wearing beads and headbands
Flowers in my head
Kids wanting to be Indian . . . but not as brown

The Summer of Love
Didn't feel like love to me
Felt like another day
Walking the streets
Grabbing something to eat and beating the heat

The Summer of Love
Seemed to be filled with hate sometimes
The thing that kept me sane
Beating the hell out of my drums
Singing my songs and fighting stage fright

Wars all around
In my house, in my world, and in my life
The Summer of Love
We need another one soon

With my buddy Steve in LA

I had always wanted to go to California. That's where the music, films, and beaches were. By the time I was nineteen, I had been banging on a kit for about five years and figured I was good enough to join the West Coast sound scene.

In November of 1971, Steve and I got on the road. Stuck our thumbs out, and in five days we were walking down Hollywood Boulevard. Our plan had been to end up in San Jose because Steve's cousin lived there. But the last car that picked us up in Missouri was heading to Los Angeles, and that's how we ended up in Hollywood. I would live in California on and off for more than twenty years.

3

A Letter to Love

On the Brooklyn Bridge, 1985

When I started pursuing music, I didn't care about anything else. I just had to get to California, that's where everything was happening. I didn't have a desire to learn about Ho-Chunk people or religion. I had my head set only on music and becoming the best drummer I could be. But then my focus shifted. In California, what I once believed was my calling shifted into something that brought me closer to who God wanted me to be. In the mid-'80s, I volunteered to go serve in New York as part of a mission trip. During my time there, I left music behind and started talking with people. Focusing on the people around me, not just the music I wanted to make. My purpose had expanded. I learned that I liked to meet people and hear their stories. I wanted to know what made them into the person standing in front of me.

That time in my life changed me for the better, and I believe it started me on my journey toward writing about myself and the people around me.

Radio Waves Goodbye

The radio put me to sleep
One ear held down pillows
While the other sent the message
To my head
Not paying attention
To what was going on
Too busy reaching for that
Same dream
The one that leaves
As soon as I recognize
It's about her and how she
Left me here
Rolling over and imagination
Fights hard to get back in
To where it feels safe
Tucked away deep into
Those same pillows
The ones that were so cheap
I bought three
Without blinking an eye
Never giving a thought
To what they held for me
And how they
Bailed me out
Time after time

Funny,
I never think of this
Stuff during the day
While I'm walking with you
And trying to determine
What we should have for lunch

A day after my friend Steve and I landed in California in 1971, we met some friends we knew from Wisconsin. They invited us to a church up in the hills. It was there that my friend and I were found by the Lord Jesus.

Glory

On our knees
We found our way
Not like the world was showing us
Not about money or fame or music
It was about our future
Our lives
And our souls
The gospel changed me and Steve forever
We may have lost our way a bit down through the years
But God who is rich in mercy
Didn't let us get out of reach
GLORY

A Letter to Love

Everyone is looking for you
You show up once in a while
They say when we aren't looking
That's what they say
You always hurt when you show up

I actually don't believe that
But you never know
If just around the corner, you wait

I didn't meet you 'til I saw you in her
Poor Indian kid woke up that day
Never felt this kind of love
So honest and true
Innocent soul that dropped from the sky
All I can do is wonder why

They say you are the most important thing to people
But I'm not sure if everyone agrees
You seem to like to hide from us
Showing up when you feel like it

You must feel good when someone finds you
The only barometer is the heart

Trainhead

The train that took you
Far away that night
The one that
Constantly wakes me up
Shakes my world
Like clockwork
Never thought I'd
Know it like this
Up close and personal
Tearing me apart
Hoping this is
Just a dream
Wake me up soon
Before I board
This constant reminder
That runs its course
Through the tunnel
I call my head
Station agents
Out to lunch
Never there
When you need them
Tickets torn
In two on floors
Like the heart
That gets swept away

Running

Ran away from home
To be with you
I took all my books
That I never read
Hoping to one day
When I get the time
Look good for you
Like I have a brain somewhere in this head
That never shows up when I need it
No matter how
Hard I try
Not impressed
With pretending idiots
Willing to change
Nothing about themselves
So much like myself
Alone and posing
For the ones who think
I am more than what I am
Sorry, folks, for the show
That always ends the same
Me alone and broken hearted

Blue Eyes

Blue eyes
The ones that used to melt me
Kept my heart in tune
While singing a different song
And me, gone for so long . . .
Memories never left
For all that time spent
Years and tears may have separated us
But not for long
In the scheme of things
Like starting over
With the one I thought I lost
Only for a moment
Somehow we made it back
Revisiting our youth
Stepping back in time
Lost for words . . .
And at times my thoughts
The memory stayed with me

I still love her

Magnet Dream

Magnetic poetry
Sticking to no one
But you
Twenty-something
Bullshit
Once again
Unnoticed
No one interested in
Your little life
And the world that
Greets us
When we reach
For the butter
Keep it to
Yourself
On the door
Of your heart
Hoping someone looks twice
Don't count
On it

Melts on Sidewalk

First time I saw you
Melted
Like ice cream
Spilt on sidewalks
Summer
Gathered myself
Enough to say hello
You said goodbye
Like winter
Freeze me
Should have
Walked
Forgot about
The chance I'm taking
Every time
My stupid brain
Tells me
This is the one
The one
That needs me

No one's in need
In this fast
One shot wicked
Trample the heart
Of the sucker
Thicket
When will we learn?

Traffic

I should have seen
The green, yellow, red
Distinctly embedded
Now in my head
Rhythm and rhymes
Left me that quick
As soon as I turned
To look at you
Exiting memories
Fought to stay on
This lonely heartache
Attached all around
Lifelines met asphalt
Shook hands and talked
How I was a loser
Shouldn't have walked
Speeding with cell phone
She never saw
The blur that was me
Lost in herself
Nineteen and hurried
By the worlds we are in
Never-ending cycle
Where love and hate win

Ships

The number of times
You cross my mind, endless
Sailing across what's left of me
Ships that take you
Into the night
Waving me goodbye
The wreck that lies
On the bottom of my heart
Slowly rusts away
Turning back to dust

May Day

That day in May
Two years have gone by fast
One day I was holding this pure, innocent, and lovable soul
In my unworthy hands, and the next thing I know
I'm at her second birthday, snapping pictures of my most favorite baby
There have been babies in my life before but none that touched me like Isabel
She was the most beautiful thing I have ever seen
The most beautiful thing I have ever held
Tears filled my heart when the true meaning of love
Rested against my chest
I looked at her like she was my own
I loved her like she was sent from Heaven above
And maybe that is what I needed
To get my heart to open to more than myself
As she grew, our time together was lovely
The way she smiled at me when I read to her
The way she laughed and that smile that always melted me
I hope she will remember me long after I'm gone
I will always remember her
And how she caused my heart to feel a love that moves me to tears

Old Friends

We met long ago
She was with another
And I wished I was
I knew it at the time
That I would love her always
It was hard to imagine one day
She would be left alone
Broken, blue, and lonely
I was sad to hear that he had left her
They were a perfect pair
Meant to be together
They say that's part of life
But it seems hard to imagine
A world where lovers leave too soon
If he hung around for a thousand years
They would have still said that

I'll be a friend and more if she lets me

Down the Street

You live down the street
I wish I saw you there

On the street where we used to live
It looks the same as it did back then

Lonely eyes see how it's changed
I look for that one that used to laugh
In the green space behind your heart

It's a lonely piece of ground now
Waiting for the love to return

Just in time to heal the land
As the heart still breaks at night

Wish I never left
Another thoughtless mistake
That I live with everyday

How can someone be so stupid?
To leave the one they love

Shelter of Wings

Time away has shown a lot about us
And who we are
If what we had was true
Or just a quick dream
We wake when we see our hearts
In the daytime
Suns come out, hiding our hurt
Hoping nightfall will protect
What we feel
Maybe it was a dream
And now we have to wake
Reality seeps back in
When we open our eyes
Sleep hides us again
How long 'til we face the truth
It's over now
We'll go on our way
Looking for what we already have
Love and listen
To what it has to say
Go back
To where you once were
Hiding under its
Sheltering wings

Enjoying a sunset and a smoke on a balcony in New Mexico in 2007

As I get older, I find myself thinking more about the past. I don't remember much about my childhood. I sometimes wish I did. I'm sure there are many good memories that I can't get to.

Looking back, I wish I had learned more about my parents and grandparents. I never thought to press them for stories of traditions or customs. To be honest, as a kid growing up in the 1950s and '60s, I wasn't interested in those things. Now I would welcome those stories and histories. I regret not knowing the language and the responsibilities of the Bear Clan, of which I am a member. I left Wisconsin in 1971 and did not return until 1995, so I was away from our tribal ways for many years.

But even when I was away, I was always thinking about home. Coming back, being surrounded by relatives and friends, listening to their stories of how they were raised—it made me want to know more. Everybody has a story.

4

The Tracks We Leave

Sam Blowsnake, my grandma Stella's older brother and my great uncle

I understand that tradition is the passing down of culture and customs from generation to generation, especially orally. This description could not be more accurate concerning us, the Ho-Chunk people. We have our beginnings right here in Wisconsin. We are said to have originated at Red Banks, on the south shore of Green Bay. That is what the stories that I have been told say.

We have many things that cannot be spoken about. They are ours, and we have learned to guard them. We have been taught to celebrate life and share with our loved ones the stories we have heard from those who have gone on. We are who we are. We are here and now. We don't know what is ahead for us, but I believe we will be able to face whatever comes our way. Our ancestors did, and so will we.

Back in the Day

Back in the day
My people always made their way
They came at a time
When hard work was an everyday thing
It's what they had to do to survive—
A way of life
We picked berries to make a few bucks
We lived among the trees
We hunted for our meals
And somehow raised our kids
To be friends of the Earth
Family love and caring kept us close
Speaking the only language we knew
The one that is in danger of leaving us now
The world wants us all to sound the same
We will never feel that way
We came from the Earth
From the dust we were formed
It's all we can do to protect what is left
We ate what the earth gave us
We weren't full of sickness and disease
We are a strong people
That believed we would survive
A strong people will always find a way
Eat well and speak the truth

Losing My Head

Short stories for free
The sign outside read
I decided to go in
Looking for my head
Behold, there it stood
Never looking so good
Can I have it back
But without the hood?
I thought you were done with it for now
Take it away don't ask me how
If you ever come back
We'll throw your ass out
We got all we could
From that opening spout
I hope they didn't take
The one thing I miss
The memory of you
And that very first kiss

Bear Boy

Bear Boy came the way we all do
The Red Stork stuttered as he left him there
On the door of the heart of the fifteen-year-old
Who cried like she never cried before
Alone once again having to care
For someone who needed it more
The life that was left
Crying and punching
His way into this world

Bloodlines in anger, embattled warfare
The world welcomed only for a moment
Turns it back quickly as soon as we need it

Two struggles
Brewing
Native life stewing
Called out to combat
The littlest soldier
Red skinned warrior
What are the chances
Of him making it?

An Indian Poem

They want me to Injun it up
To speak of the Earth and Moon
And all the animals that walk it
I should really show the Indian me
That's where the bucks are, they said
Whites wanna know about you guys

But I just can't go there when I sit here and type
I wish I could do the medicine man or the warrior thing
I wasn't brought up that way
My folks let me be what I wanted
A brown guy who fell in love with music
When I saw mop tops sing like no one else

I know it's not what you wanna hear

My dad was raised in Winnebago, Nebraska, and attended Winnebago High School in the late 1930s. He was a talented athlete and played on the basketball team that won the state championship in 1940. The school didn't win another championship until seventy-five years later.

Winning All Alone

In this day and age
When all the world
Cheers for heroes
Kids today are raised to hate the zeroes
It wasn't always like that
For a bunch of ballers
Straight out of the Rez
With no pro team callers
No big crowds around to cheer
For Indian boys with little to fear
That gave all they got to get to the top
Truly they were hard to stop
Despite the odds that were against them
They played like they were on the biggest stage
High school ballers
Made the history page
They played hard in the title fight
Like the world was watching Lakers ball
Battled like warriors
Skinny legs and all
160 and 20 the record said

That was the way they made their way
To the big dance 100 miles away
The gym was small and hardly full
But they were used to crowds that small
Back then they had no pull
No parade to greet the bus
That pulled in later that night
They only knew they won the fight
Don't know if they cut down nets
That lonely winter night
All they knew was
Indian boys had won another fight
Seven decades later in 2015
Red boy warriors brought home another prize
Long time coming
Another big surprise

Day in Life

Mornings whisper
Skies that echo
What it says
The arrival of day
Another chance
To live this life
The one that's
Given us
All that it has
Tears and hurt
Love and joy
What it is
That makes us
Who we are
Directions taken
In a moment
Right or wrong
Living with it
Don't ponder
Too long
It moves by fast
When we aren't looking
Hopeful

By the evening
When the stars
Tuck us in
For the night
Readying
For another
Chance
To make it right

Fishing Petenwell

One of those days
I wish there were more
A good day to show my skills on the
Cold Wisconsin shore
It felt good to show up
My dad and his bro
Cane pole angler
Had more to show
The lures that they bought
Didn't do the trick
Don't try to whip me
With my worms on a stick
My dad and his brother
Left us too soon
The fish were happy
When they finished their tune
The water all around me
Moves along slowly
Fish and things dance softly
Maybe they don't know me

I wrote this after I visited the home of my Cuuwi, JoAnn Jones, which was filled with art, pictures, and a room full of memories. Many Ho-Chunk homes are like this—maybe a designer's nightmare, but to me a thing of beauty, our lives and memories hanging in front of us, surrounding us.

Walls That Talk

The ones that are filled with love
They talk to her everyday
Letting her know she'll be okay
At night they watch over her
Whispering her favorite words and songs
Melodies that will never fade
As long as she keeps them close
They all hold hands as they keep watch
Bound together by love and care
Never going anywhere
Till the time they turn to dust
Back into the Universe

Coasting

I may be broken
In two or three pieces
Maybe more
I can't tell
'Til the pain pill
Releases

I can only
Sit back and wait
Hoping I'm wrong
Up for debate

Love is cruel
Tearing the masses
Like earthquakes emotions
Hold on 'til it passes

Don't take my word
Find out yourself
Fault lines don't lie
California's on shelves

Falling away
Inevitable, they say
From the rest of the world
Get out of the way

Landslides are lonely
Coastlines cry out
Hitting rock bottom
Without any doubt

Whatever the weather
We're under it all
Waves crash at night
We are so small

Looking Behind

Oh, he's Indian
The little voice
Said from behind me
I can tell by his hair
And the cheeks
Dead giveaways
The bones of a Redman
Aged and sun drenched
Telling my story
Of life
And love entrenched
Holding on tightly
Of what's left of our story
Keeping it close
Won't give ya the gory
Details of tribes' battles
Losing ourselves—
That we can't handle
So look at us now
While you can before we go
Lonely red lives
Barking at heels

We've danced the last tango
Do you still wanna be us?
Along with the baggage
Wards of the state
Take out the garbage

In 2017, I was accepted to the University of New Mexico. I took acting and playwriting classes. I lived on the third floor of an apartment building that faced west, and every night I was treated to a beautiful sunset. I liked it there because of the food, the views, and all the brown people.

New Mexico

The blood-red sunset
Said it all last night

One sweep of Nature's brush
Broad stroked my mind
Raced thunder to get away
The rain that fell soon after
Dripped on me like the others

Left alone again
Sandstone memories
Monuments of shame
Built when I wasn't looking

Red rock image
Never meant much to tone deaf profits

The rocks from whence I came
Or the wind that blew her in

Indigenous follower, aimless archer
She is like the rest of them
Looking for good times

Deceived by her own stars

Two A.M.

It's two a.m. and night falls on me hard
I should be used to it by now
Lying here alone with my thoughts
It's been going on for a long time
But it always somehow feels new
When it shows up to greet me
I look back on the life that I've led
All the ups and downs
The good and the bads
The memories that keep me up nights
The way I hurt
And the way I hurt others
Especially the ones I loved
I wish I could go back
To when I was good
When I was in touch with the one who made me
I only hope I can get back there
And once again find favor

Me and the Jukebox

Being a young singer
Or thinking I was one
All by myself on the barroom floor
Or at least feeling that way when I walk in the door
Eating cheap burgers and watching my dad
Laughing and smiling with Friday night's team
I didn't remember too much around me
Except for the sounds of the Wurlitzer circles
Making my way into my head via sound waves
Somehow reaching my ten-year-old heart
Making me think of things I never knew
It echoed through my head, telling the story
Of loved ones and losing
Trucks and beer and cheating cowboys and cowgirls
Not a word about Indians or how their lives were
We had stories about love and about leaving
Driving trucks and drinking
Fighting and singing
I guess they didn't write those
Back in the day
Not enough info, I guess
Or maybe nobody cared about how Red lives were
To tell you the truth
I didn't care either. I was trying to remember lyrics
Something to think about fifty years later
The songs that hummed me every time I hear them
Fifty years passed and now present with me
Still hums in my head when I think of those days

Every hillbilly story and love line told
I recall the songs I liked and the ones that stuck with me
It always brings me back to those days
Baseball cleats clacking on rough wooden floors
The smell of beer and cigarette smoke
Those days with my mom and pops
I miss them a lot
Every time
I sing in the shower

Black River

The month was May
When arriving that day
The homeland of my people
They had been there for ages
From what I am told
They were moved out West
The government wanted them out
Some of us made it back
Many did not

The river they called Black
Just like some of the times for my people
It wasn't easy back in the day
Race and hate were all around

My dad was away
So with Grandma we stayed
Her little home in what's known as the Mission
I remember the little white house
It's not there anymore
Just like many people that I loved

Time flies by and people come and go
Many names I can't remember
When I walk through the family cemetery
They rest there now

White Guy Drums

She asked me if I do the powwow thing
After I told her I was a drummer, trying to impress

And I do mean I was a drummer
A darn good one many moons ago
When I still had hair
She asked me why I didn't drum the Injun drum
I told her because white guy drums rock more
Oh, my Native homies did freak out when I said that

She laughed and walked away
I never did get her name

Dammit . . . story of my life

Sleep Story

Forced to write
About my life's story
Ups and downs
Of a fool and his dream
No one has interest
As plots thicken daily
Wakened too soon
Before the show ended
Ruined again
By the softness that
Follows
Pillows of sleep
Get in my way

The World Today

We care little for the lives around us
Chasing the dollar bill that owns us

And all the things it can buy
Votes and souls, we wonder why

Is it really that important?
To lie and steal and destroy it

Why can't we see that life is more
Than being another money whore

It makes the best of us turn bad
Greed and lies we never had

The downside of gaming money
Greed takes over always running

Bullets tearing us apart
Families and hearts that depart

Madmen taking lives away
And leaders look the other way

When will we ever learn
That we are here for a short life term

Speck in the Sky

Standing at crossroads
Wondering which way to go
Where will we be taken
By this chance of love and luck?
The fate that steps in daily
On unknowing lovers like us
Getting sucker punched
When we weren't looking
Wondering about the truth
Of it all
If there is a truth
To discover
Maybe stars lined up
When we weren't looking
Unaware we were the ones
That were affected
A drop in the sky
A tiny speck in the
Scheme of things
We happened to be the ones
Our number was up
Like lottery dreamers
Who never win a thing
Now we cash in the ticket
Waiting in line to get paid
Small bills abound
On the poverty stricken

Confusion sinks in
Fogging our mind
Holding us down
'Til we can find
Who we really are
And if we still fit in
With the rest of the world

Old

The days are short
They go by so fast
Never thought
I'd get this far

But here I am
Old and creaky
Bones are sore all the time

Walking and bending
Giving me fits
I hear what I want to hear
And I disregard the rest

I lost my patience a while ago
Losing interest in a minute
For those who pass my way
I don't see what's in it

I used to be nice back when I had hair
Time, it moves fast

I wish I didn't care

While Bears Sleep

Winter waits for us to sleep
Growing old in whitened deep
Shivers shake us down to souls
Hibernate me from the cold
Maybe, when we rise next
Spring love will wake and take us in
Newfound dreams may find their way
Through the ice to where we stay
Down below this saddened ground
Hidden where no one's around
Lucky ones not having to deal
With human nature
And all they feel

The last time everyone in our family
was together, Christmas 1990

My parents supported me in everything I did. My dad gave everything for us kids; he was supportive even if he didn't quite understand what he was supporting. The care my parents showed our family uplifted us and allowed us to live the lives we all carry out now. Dad often told me, "Always leave them wanting more." To me that means leaving behind a story for those coming after me, leaving them wanting more for themselves, their futures, and their families.

I'm grateful for the love they gave me, as it afforded me the chance to be who I am today. We are each called to follow the tracks left by those who came before us, sometimes treading a path that is all our own, leading us toward the person we were always meant to be.

Acknowledgments

Thanks to

the Ho-Chunk Nation and the
Ho-Chunk Nation Education Department,

the University of Wisconsin–Baraboo-Sauk County
English Department,

David Cole, Ken Grant, and Bill Drennan,

the University of New Mexico Art Department,

the Wisconsin Historical Society Press staff,

and above all, my Lord Jesus.

Discussion Questions

1. Many facets of Sherman's life are unique to his experience, but others feel universal. What parts of his story did you relate to most?

2. Sherman's poems include many references to the ways in which Native people were treated in the 1960s and '70s. What aspects of Sherman's need to navigate both his Native culture and the majority white culture are most relevant to today's world?

3. Much of Sherman's life journey was driven by the desire to find home, inspiration, or companionship. Which of these themes did you find to be most prominent?

4. In this book, Sherman organizes his poems and reflections into the themes of growing up, music, relationships, and self-discovery. Discuss which of the four sections of the book you relate to most and why.

5. Talk about a specific poem, image, or line that struck you as significant. Why was it memorable to you?

6. Many of Sherman's poems consider an individual's place in their community, family, or friend group. How did this book encourage you to reflect on your own place in life and how you move through each day?

7. Sherman says that he never planned to be a writer. Now that you've read this book, do you think he is a writer? What does it take for someone to be considered a writer or a storyteller?

8. The book's final poem closes with the following lines: "Down below this saddened ground / Hidden where no one's around / Lucky ones not having to deal / With human nature / And all they feel." How does this encompass Sherman's story? In what ways do you connect with this sentiment?

9. What have you learned by reading Sherman's memoir? How has it changed or broadened your perspective or outlook?

About the Author

Sherman Funmaker is a poet, a musician, and an enrolled member of the Ho-Chunk Nation from Baraboo, Wiscons[illegible] graduating from UW–Baraboo, Funmaker began coaching and collaborating with other writers and creatives in his community. He has presented workshops on storytelling for high school students and adults. He lives in Wisconsin Dells, Wisconsin.